REUNION
SONGS

For my parents,
Maxine and Neil.

PRAISE FOR *REUNION SONGS*

"This eloquent, lyrical collection of poems reveals the nonhuman world around us in exquisite detail. We are offered a way through to our other-than-human family, to the natural world."

TRACY COTTRELL

"A deeply moving reading experience, *Reunion Songs* allows us to celebrate a very special reunion, an internal homecoming with ourselves. Each poem guides us to recognise ourselves more fully, with greater acceptance and love of our own innate natural gifts, questions and truths. Liberating, wise, unapologetic, humorous and hugely relevant in our current times, *Reunion Songs* is a gift to anyone who dares to follow their call."

KATJA ELK

"This book is an apothecary filled with remedies for the ailments of modern life. It is a guide to befriending the more trustworthy parts of ourselves and a summons to souls untethered from the truth of their own belonging. Through her poems, Amanda facilitates a homecoming by giving voice to the unnamable force which lovingly yearns for our awakening. There is a depth of spirituality contained within it that is not for the faint-hearted. We are encouraged to see, and to come to know, that the sacred is writ large through everything, even that which we wish to turn away from. Poet, mystic and translator for the unseen, Amanda delivers healing balms, powerful invocations and cosmic truths, all with the lightest of touches."

CHLOE HOPE, *DEATH & BIRDS*

"Amanda's dowsing rod is a pen tuned to spirit. Pulled by those deep currents, she leads our oldest longings to a lush and welcoming new home. I would follow her anywhere."

LARA O'CONNOR

PRAISE FOR *REUNION SONGS*

"The poems of *Reunion Songs* lift your spirits, honour your challenges and encourage both gritty persistence and surrender. Amanda's language is lyrical and unfussy, honed to an essential simplicity. Its like your best friend sharing her musings and wisdom—if your best friend also happened to be a poet."

MICHELLE SPENCER, *ARMCHAIR REBEL*

"In *Reunion Songs*, Amanda invites us inside her journey of remembering and reuniting with who she is. As you read, you can feel yourself lifting off and touching down over and over, all while coming closer to yourself. A beautiful tonic for these times of change."

MARY WALKER, *LULLABY FOR MOTHERS* AND *THE LAND WILL HOLD YOU*

"Amanda Cooke's poems wake me from slumbers I didn't know I'd fallen into—as if having been rocked to sleep by the rhythm of the train of life, her verse is the unexpected jolt that wakes me up again, causes my eyes to widen, brings me back to awareness, to the present moment, makes me sit up and pay attention once more to the beauty outside my window. Each poem in this collection will reach into your heart and invite you to follow, bringing you closer to yourself and to the love that's always within but often obscured. With a voice that's loving, curious and hungry for life, you'll be guided on an exploration of themes of home, belonging, love, self-remembrance and awakening, and you'll come away with just a little more courage to live life more boldly, more authentically and more aligned with that quiet but insistent voice within that's always beckoning you home."

EMMA CAMPBELL WEBSTER

REUNION SONGS

poems for reconnection
and remembering yourself home

AMANDA COOKE

Published in Australia by
One Sky Press
P.O. Box 3539
South Brisbane BC QLD 4101
Australia

First published in Australia 2024
Copyright © Amanda Cooke 2024

Cover design: Silke Stein
Cover artwork: *untitled* by Shane Drinkwater
Book interior: Sophie White
Author photo: Jade Ferguson

A catalogue record is available at the National Library of Australia.

NATIONAL LIBRARY OF AUSTRALIA
A catalogue record for this book is available from the National Library of Australia

ISBN 978-1-7636217-0-1 (paperback)
ISBN 978-1-7636217-4-9 (hardback)
ISBN 978-1-7636217-1-8 (limited edition hardback)
ISBN 978-1-7636217-3-2 (epub)

Printed by Ingram Spark

ONE SKY PRESS

CONTENTS

3. SONGS OF RETURN

PREFACE

As a child, I grew up free to roam. I was happiest in the company of the land and the creatures that also called my bush backyard home. I remember never feeling afraid or out of place there. Since then, I forgot much, but the memory remained, and the unnamable yearning for return only increased with my forgetting. What is lost longs to be remembered.

It wasn't until adulthood that I found myself very much outnumbered by the other-than-human world again. There, on a hill surrounded by forest in the middle of nowhere, I finally found words for the disconnection I felt and the longing I had for reunion with the wilder world, seen and unseen, that I had forgotten I belonged to.

These poems were born from that longing and from the guidance of the other-than-human world that helped me find my way. Writing them has taken me on a journey of awakening, remembering, healing and homecoming that continues and will go on unfolding. We are but a tiny tale in a limitless and unknowable story.

Many of these poems were written with singing or speaking out loud in mind, and the book itself is organised in song cycles to reflect the rhythm in which the poems arrived, the journey itself and the ancient way we humans navigated the world, intimately interwoven and in conversation with it. The book is a living map of memory and the way.

There is something alchemical about bringing to life through voice the words that live inside us or on a page, uniting heart, mind, body and soul in harmony. They are freed to roam and be in their own conversation with the world.

These poems are my way of remembering, reconnecting and reclaiming the life I always longed for without necessarily travelling anywhere. Writing them has become a sacred practice of reweaving myself back into a wilder story. Through sharing them with you, they become places for you to explore with your own knowing as your guide.

In remembering our interconnectedness, our true belonging to what the poet Mary Oliver describes as "the family of things", we begin the journey back to ourselves and each other. We are not meant to do this life alone.

My hope is that this book supports you on your path of homecoming.

1.

RECONNECTION
SONGS

THE ATTRACTION

Drop the song that won't be sung.
Come, fall back in love with the world instead.
Can you feel my breath on your neck?

I miss you.

HOMECOMING

Lay down your questions, drop your bow,
yield to nothing if you dare.
The space between stories is yours to know.

Time melts, lost with no place to go,
only silence, a moment stripped bare
when you lay down your questions, drop your bow.

Forms merging, converging, no above or below.
We are one, breath ripples to air
in the space between stories that is yours to know.

Kin calls, *Come bathe in the eternal flow.*
Remember, truth waits for you there
when you lay down your questions, drop your bow.

Heart listens, takes flight, ecstatic, aglow
in between worlds with gifts to share
from the space between stories that is yours to know.

Your homecoming shatters the status quo,
now freed from conclusion, beyond despair.
When you lay down your questions, drop your bow,
the space between stories isn't hard to know.

INHERITANCE

1.
Loosen your grip,
lie down with me now.
The space between stories is yours to know.
For better or worse, the world is still beautiful.
There is nowhere else to be but here,
feeling for each other,
remembering how to be kin.

2.
When the ocean beckons you,
greet her with your loving cup.
Feel the wind's call, let him
hear your cry back.
What aches in you
longs for you too

for the dead are not dead.
Be unafraid, make amends
then pray for the living.
Remember how to love.

Know you need not be
chosen, grieving or good
to inherit, to belong in this world.
All it takes is your very first breath.

ONE DAY SOON

One day soon when you wake up
and realise all you've been told is a lie,
the ground will not fall away beneath you.
You will drop to your knees and give thanks
for how it catches your every step.
You will marvel at the invisible
companionship of your breath,
how your gaze reveals everything
once hidden in plain sight.

May you have the courage to face
the immensity of your absence.

May it unlock your heart and let it
be flooded with the infinite welcoming
of the here and now.

There is a new song being sung.

May its music find you and keep you.
May you revel and sing in the miracle
of your glorious ordinaryness.

MYSTERY

Mystery

make me an instrument of the unseen,
guide me between worlds;
I long to know the wild edge of life.
For too long my heart was a prisoner
of my mind until I dared taste
your offerings of freedom.
I am ready now
to be a student of Truth,
learn the tongues of the Cosmos,
read the seed stories of my Soul.

Mystery

grant me the courage to roam the vast plains in search of truth with the faith I will never be lost.

Grant me the fearlessness to feel the fullness of love, knowing I also risk its inextricable loss.

Grant me the compassion to hold all parts of myself tenderly and the grace to give mercy to those not yet ready to love all of themselves.

Grant me the serenity to see that even in chaos I will always have my soul as compass.

Grant me the humility to know that I am but one drop and the wisdom to know I am also the whole ocean.

Mystery

make me an instrument of the unseen.
Show me the way home.

2.

SONGS OF
REMEMBERING

BEFORE SLEEP

What if rest was the real work,
that when you sleep you take flight,
a night bird navigating by moonlight
through all that was and ever will be?

To live into/your infinite potential is to have faith.
Every night you surrender to this
journey through the realms of your soul
where only they have the map.

Trust them to chart a course through that world
towards what calls you in this one,
to retrieve everything lost and longed for,
to make the invisible visible in your dreams.

Before sleep, remember:
all that is required is your readiness.

I am here, night flyer. Tell me what you know.

Then promise on waking you will
remember to weave what was given
back into this world
so when it calls you here,
it captures your attention
long enough for you to wonder
if, like distant thunder,
a change is coming.

HOW TO DIVE BACKWARDS

You can do it sight unseen.
Fingers know—trust them.
They hold your fear and promise.
Lie back now, heart undone, reaching,
eyes open or closed, no matter,
the same water rises to greet you,
the only difference surprise
and a multitude of lives.

STILLNESS

Close your eyes,
let me be companion to your aloneness.
We are in the unseen world now,
all you need is willingness.
I am the emptiness, I am the way.

Lift your ear to me, listen.
I am your dreaming, your trembling,
your bridge between worlds.
Anchor yourself in me,
I am the ground to your uprising.

When you are lost in me, remember
you are born from darkness.
Have faith, feel for me,
rising and falling to our moon; know
we are fellow travellers wed to the stars.

STEERING BY STARLIGHT

I close my eyes hoping to find you,
a trace of treasure on a barren ocean.

Compass in hand, I plot a course
with hardly a hint of you

then, in a splash, you are there.
I scramble for my net, but you're gone

not lost, just swallowed by sea,
unseen until I catch another glimpse

on arrival at that distant shore,
only to discover the mere ghost of you

so I journey on, steering by starlight,
knowing there are infinite ways to navigate God.

CAST AWAY

Before you know it
something will come
without warning or mercy.
With no list at hand
of what must be saved
even your breath will
be taken from you.

Woe betide you try
to flee with nowhere
to hide and no higher ground.
Against some things
there is no defending
only succumbing
to life underwater.

One thing is certain:
in the end you will
find refuge, cast away,
free of falsehoods,
laid bare again
on the clean-swept
shore of your life.

HOLDING YOU HOLDING ME

ode to my coffee cup

What's it like holding everything and nothing at all,
to know that as you empty, my world rushes in?

Do you know that when I hold your heaviness in my hands,
you are holding mine too?

A tsunami can swell within your walls.

You are so much more than your usefulness,
my safe haven, voyage keeper, partner in crime.
My rescuer from not enough time.

You see, you shape me as I once shaped you
with your tiny rebellions against sameness
in spite of the wheel that turned you.

Even now, when you are empty
you become my morning offering to the world,
my reminder that I am ready.

NIGHT WATCH

When you wake to the taste of blood
from another night of fighting,
know that your warrior fell fearlessly on the field
of dreams without mourning or memory.

Day or night, nothing lasts. Even so,
don't lose heart, nor is it lost or wasted,
rather returned and recycled,
turned for eternity into the dreaming.

So much is out of your command:
beauty, terror. Beware of claiming credit,
it has less to do with you than you know.
All you can do is be tender with yourself,
allow days to break and mend again.

Lick your wounds now, caress your jaw,
hold yourself for a moment and remember
beneath your armour is a guardian who never sleeps.
Let them take watch, be relieved from your duty.
Dare to be held, and behold vigilance fall.

THREE GENTLE REMINDERS

and a Not So Gentle Nudge

1.

For you who woke feeling defeated,
you cannot lose at your own life.
In the game of comparison
the house always wins.
Walk. Away.
I see your fierce heart.
You are braver than you think.

2.

For you who woke feeling trapped,
it is never too late to reclaim your own life.
You are wilder, more glorious than you know.
I trust your soaring/yearning heart.

3.

For you who woke in despair,
remembering to breathe is easier said than done.
Instead, look up and remember
everything changes, even this.
This is the breath that will save you.

AND A NOT SO GENTLE NUDGE

Yes, my love,
life is slipping through your fingers.
Loosen your grip now.

You can't drink from a clenched fist.

TAKE ME TO THE RIVER

Lay me down, hold me,
show me how to yield,
knowing I can drown in you.

Lift me up, move me,
help me how to remember
all the ways love can save me.

WHEN IN PAIN

Pain is a messenger. Listen.
Beware of the *more this, less that* kind,
the kind that demands
be different, do better, try harder,
the shouty false prophet
with the nasty aftertaste.

Pain is a messenger. Listen
closer for the *I am here, walk with me* kind,
the kind that says *I know your worth,*
let me carry the full weight of your despair,
the whispering invitation back to love
with the sweetness of freedom.

FALL

How do you know when it's time?

Is it the first brush of wind or
the fullness of that last kiss
of rain on your dry skin?

Have you no fear of falling?

Too deep in rapture of the dance
to notice your fall into grace.
Like a shooting star,
in a gasp you are gone,
your sacrifice only glimpsed
from the corner of my eye.

WHEN FEAR COMES

When fear comes promising security,
wearing masks of envy and blame,
listen for love's quiet truth in uncertainty.

The risks of trust—hurt, complexity—
overwhelm, bully and shame
when fear comes promising security.

In stillness lie the answers, clarity,
ignition of your heart's flame.
Listen for love's quiet truth in uncertainty.

Step gently in beauty and possibility,
know your soul that dread can't tame,
when fear comes promising security.

Life is a sacred dance of simplicity.
With an open heart you play the game.
Listen for love's quiet truth in uncertainty.

Peace comes not on open palms of surety;
belonging is yours to claim.
When fear comes promising security,
listen for love's quiet truth in uncertainty.

WAITING ROOM

You wondered as you waited

What would I do if I wasn't afraid?
Would I whisper 'Why not me?' and mean it?

Then, below the whirlpool of worries,
you glimpsed treasure buried within you,
a sea unfathomable and still
untouched by the ripples of mere words.

What will be will always be. Now
between the swirl and the sea is me.
Fierce.
Free.

THE SEA IN ME

When I stand on your shore
an ocean rises in me,
sweeping me clean then
swamping me with truth,
the true order of things.

Like a lover lost at sea returned,
the desire to weep is a reminder
it is not my job to be good
but just to be here, to
allow myself to be moved.

THE SEA IS NOT
MADE OF WATER

Sometimes, most times,
moving on means first
being drawn far out to sea
where time quickens
then crests and turns
in on itself,
neither held
nor free.

One gasp is all you have
to glimpse the vast mystery
that carries you before
the crash and pull swallows
then lays you bare again
on the shore of your life.

Can you see now
the sea is not made of water
but tiny worlds, lost and remade,
time and again by mightier
forces than you?

EASE

Many rivers flow into the same sea.
Do not let this truth keep you from living
or blind you to what you cannot see.
You have no idea where you are going.

Let yourself be led by the flow in you
that knows and greets the other openly.
Remember the ease of this meeting of waters
who recognise each other as their own.

ON WAKING

When you wake with a tired heart,
know that the world needs this too.
It longs for your joy and your sorrow.

You, now, here in this bed,
the dawn rousing you into being,
this is your reminder to remember.

Know that you know your fullest magnitude
and how it feels when it calls you;
this is all that matters.

Just as you were carried unawares
from that world into this,
released into the bed of morning,

you know how to send shoots and roots
through the darkness,
to trust in the unfolding of what you cannot see.

When you wake, remember
you are not the seed or the flower.
You are the unfurling and the uprising,

life itself,
visible for a brief moment
in bloom.

WHEN WAITING

While I hang around here circling,
waiting for a change in the wind,
I wonder how seabirds do it,
navigating by nose and knowing,
tracking the turning north and south,
no questions, no doubts, just ride or die.
For them there's no such thing as a holding pattern,
only strong and steady, flap and glide.
Even when static they're soaring.

THE WAY

Drop the map,
lift your finger to the wind.
The sun and moon long
to conspire in your unfolding.

No matter the push or pull
of shoulds and coulds,
the inner tide of your breath
falls and rises to your moon.

Let today be the day
you plot with what's written inside you
to turn towards what nourishes.
Trust it to help guide you too.

FAITH

On days when impatience pulls you
too early out of yourself
towards who you long to be,
you risk tightening the very knots
you've worked so hard to loosen.

I'm not asking you to give up,
just to let yourself be now and then
to make room for more
dexterous forces than us.

How quickly we forget that coming
undone has its own unknowable magic.
Such divine disentanglement
can never be seen or hurried,
only forsaken with leaps of faith.

WILD HOPE FOR BLEEDING HEARTS

WHEN I CAN'T RECOGNISE THE WORLD, I close my eyes and dream of one not gone blind. I try to remember everything I've forgotten, like how to eat without biting off more than I can chew or needing always to swallow the lump in my throat. I remember how to wail with my whole self without fear it will kill me.

They say we were made for these broken times, and yet most days, in a blind world, my bleeding heart feels unfit for purpose, so I close my eyes and dream of a not-blind world, where I go to remember. Where I also go to forget.

When I take root in this sighted world, I don't need clues to live or for every feather that falls at my feet to be a personal message from God. In this world where there are no rules, I am content to be reckless, a channel for chaos, a desire path for beasts.

In this world I remember how to be barefoot, that I was made to walk a million miles for love in a broken, blind world, so that when I can't recognise the world, I remember to close my eyes and remember me, barefoot in a not-blind world and not forget.

ON HARD DAYS

On days when hopelessness reigns,
remember, you came here
to love and to liberate.
In a sea of indifference,
be an island of tiny kindnesses,
each an illumination of the truth
of our belonging to each other.

On hard days, find that part of you
that longs to love more.
Stay close to it, let it lead.
Light up, let yourself
be found, otherwise
how will we ever find our way
back to each other?

NOT DARK YET

What would the old ones do
if they knew darkness was coming?
I cup my hand to my ear,
waves crash against my palm,
I listen for/hear what is hidden.

When the curlew cries into the night,
remember they descend from heirs
of the fall of an ancient age of kings,
ones who also loved and lost a world
then offered themselves to the wind.

Until then we must tend the garden,
love all the children, share tea,
go on in the world as we find it.
We keep it worth living in, otherwise
what would we do for solace then?

HOW TO HELP

When waters in you rush up
to quench a thirsty world,
wait

take a moment to sink
deep down into your well,
cup your hand to your heart,
drink

let your beat and breath
find and fill you first.

Only then surge
from source to surface
so that when you can do
nothing you have
at least saved yourself.

Look at you now,
a cup and a spring,
rising and falling,
flowing freely
not flooding.
Filling cups,
never running dry.

BORN SPINNING

When the lawlessness
leaves you reeling,
know what truly moves you.
Tethered to turning,
the call of the moon,
you were born spinning.
Let yourself be danced.

You carry oceans,
bleed nights, birth days.
Know you are the echo,
the true order of things,
shattered stardust, mystery
expanding/contracting,
collapsing in cosmic embrace.

EVERYDAY ECSTASY

Every now and again
what you didn't know you wanted
collides with itself, disarming delusion
to reveal something so alive
it will not be bound.

This is life having its sweet way with you.

Don't waste precious time with words.
Be played, neither string nor music,
for a brief moment.
You are delight dancing
freed from form, writhing
in raptures with life
before you are lost
once again
to the depths
of your own
imaginings.

RECLAMATION SONG I

Born on mighty waves
crashing to shore,
don't be afraid when they
come to reclaim you.
You know how to yield
what can't be denied.

Salt waters hunger for home.
Let yourself be overcome.

Joy and grief will take
you over and over,
crashing and crying,
longing for consummation.
You know how to yield
what can't be denied.

Salt waters hunger for home.
Let yourself be overcome.

Heaving vastness releasing,
reclaiming grain by grain,
you are life renewing,
leaving hunger for salt.
You know how to yield
what can't be denied.

Salt waters hunger for home.
Let yourself be overcome.
Salt waters hunger for home.
Let yourself be overcome.

LIVING SONG

I've lived in ordinary places
at unimportant times,
longing for tomorrow,
waiting for a sign.

I've never found the time or place
to meet that appetite.
Life is an insatiable mystery
known by magic not by might.

There are no rules to follow,
only sing out *I am here!*
then pay attention closely,
to what falls into your ear.

This life is a precious gift,
one long leaving and return.
Take your sweet time, my love.
There is so much to unlearn.

You are living song, a prayer
ancient and not written,
born to know and to dare,
to echo through the ether.

IT'S TIME

freedom song

It's time, craft a nest
from those sticks and stones.

It's time, shake yourself off now.
This moment is an open window.

That sweet smell of rain,
birds singing your name.
You know we are all born lucky.

It's time, let your wish
bone fly you home.

Let your wishbone
fly you home.

Open your throat.
Now go.

IN THE END

Finally, when what was
held tight in the bud
for so long bursts open,
there will be no containment.
There is nothing more unstoppable
than a hidden truth breaking free.

Have you ever seen the Sun
take the sky so thoroughly,
cleaving the blackest clouds open,
waters rupturing, or Earth
ripped apart, reclaiming what
was theirs all along?

Against all odds and obstacles,
life in pursuit of itself persists,
and in the end
many things will break.

Let them.

3.

SONGS OF
RETURN

RESTORATION SONG

It only takes a moment
to change everything and nothing,
all you need is your noticing.

The world knows you more
intimately than you could ever imagine.
Nothing and no one is denied her embrace,
not even you.

Take off your shoes now,
you, here in this body.
The body of the Earth
rising up to meet you, saying *yes*.
This is where you belong.

It's never too late to remember
what you've been waiting for,
that it only takes a moment to mend a life.

IT'S NEVER TOO LATE

I want to know the world,
know that I belong to it

to stand on the land of my ancestors,
breathe in their forgotten journeys

ride a horse bareback, wild,
unafraid, married to the moment

to know surrender freely given
not coerced by despair.

Most of all, I long to remember my own song,
sing it uninvited, every note a lament and reunion.

What have I got to lose?
The undoing of a well-made life?

It's never too late
to name what longs to be named

abide exile no more,
to throw open

the window of your life
and gasp in amazement.

THE KISS

Kiss me,
not just the way lovers do
with lips and limbs.
Take me down through the bones
to where our rivers meet,
our only vows
to behold and be held,
to be swept out to sea.
We are travellers on the tides,
pulled hard by one moon,
scooped up and rained down
upon the world
time and time again.

NOT SO PURE NOW

Once upon a time
I was a lionbird,
all risk and infinity
reaching running
galactic wind
cascading mountain

I'm much less pure now,
more molten amphibian
fifty shades of angry horny
submarine volcano
1968 tectonic mustang.

NOW YOU ARE GONE

You were one of the good ones,
strapping, unpredictable,
the best kind of mountain.
A rebel ship in the night,
you would arrive
always with a book,
waking, shaking me up,
a reminder and a warning,
love and honour constant
through your contradictions.

Now you are gone, will you still visit me?
My dreams will always be a safe place to land.
Know I will wait for you there.

LOVE

Believe it or not,
after the final breaking
I am not dead.

I fall softly now,
from tongue to ear,
tongue to ear,
ripening, never old.
An ancient song,
I come alive
in your longing.

Can you see
in this quick embrace
we are still dancing?

EVERYDAY APPARITIONS

In the distance I see an old man
hauling his life behind him,
then there you are,
your signature bounce
in voice and stride,
all in beside him,
no pity or performance.

I smile, he laughs,
then you're gone,
back to wherever you folks go
when you leave us behind,
until the next time
you know we need
a reminder to breathe.

RECLAMATION SONG II

an ode to leaf litter

Under my feet
you sing your song of reclamation.

How must it be to know everything and nothing at all,
only sunlight, flight and sweet soil,
the seasons and pulse of inevitability?

An eternal reverie of
decay

        digestion

            alchemy

                revival.

In my hands I trace your veins.
You sing me the stories of the universe.

ETERNAL RIVER

Born from yearning
into a river of forgetting,
upstream is now a dream.
Oblivious to my fate,
I flow and forget,
purely for the joy
of remembering.

MOTHER TONGUE

From under your skirt I glimpse the world,
your leafy arms reaching, keeping it all
just out of grasp, quiet enough for me
to hear your tongue without names.
What I don't know, I try to understand.

I remember speaking without words
when the feel of the stick in my small hand
told me that if I held it just right it held
that dirt would give way with the right touch.
I knew every branch that held and broke me.

I remember knowing who was watching
without seeing and to not be afraid,
instead to let you keep me company,
showing me I wasn't a stranger,
just another source of wonder.

Now here I am in your lap with my morning coffee.
I take off my shoes, rest my bare feet on yours,
hoping for a quiet revelation to take root in me.
I close my eyes and listen for the old gods
speaking my mother tongue.

WHEN THE WIND SAYS DANCE

tree song

Some say there is no other way,
that we must pick a side.
Before I knew myself as a tree,
I might have believed them.
Now I know if that were really true,
we may as well already be dead.

Now I have ears to the ground and stars,
I hear those calling for the other way.

They say I am no stranger to ruin
or being pulled apart by panic.
I know how to stand up,
make poison into blessing,
to break in two and survive.
I know how to cling to life
with a heart laid bare.
I know the depths of my courage,
the depths of my courage.

I hold time and seeds of a new world,
I know what is lost when we forget.
We belong to each other.
I cannot be desensitised,
only expand in widening circles,
resuscitate and be shelter,
bear witness and give thanks,
say yes when the wind says dance.

I hold time and seeds of a new world,
I know what is lost when we forget.
We belong to each other.
I will not be desensitised,
only expand in widening circles,
resuscitate and be shelter,
bear witness and give thanks,
say yes when the wind says dance.

Say yes when the wind says dance.
Say yes when the wind says dance.
Say yes when the wind says dance.
Say yes when the wind says dance.

THE SHAPE OF WINGS

Inside me lives a bird
so fine sometimes I fear
they must surely be dead,
crushed by my despairing.
Today, though, I soar at the
touch of wingtips tickling my edges,
both of us expanding and contracting in harmony,
my back bowed, shoulder blades spread ready,
hoping they won't take flight without me.

Some of us spend our whole/entire lives on ground,
others never land, but one thing is certain:
there is pleasure in wings the wee bird knows
that we may never understand—to meet
the world not just by rising
but by reaching and resting,
ethereal and earthbound,
losing and finding balance,
over and over again.

ALONE

When I spend time alone
I am never lonely.
In fact, I keep company
with outlaws and angels
in the far reaches of me.
Here, I am not awkward,
broken or a stranger.
I am weightless, free,
still enough to hear the land,
sea and sky speak to me.
In this place I do not
jump at every little thing
or fight the magic. I am
never hungry or afraid.
I am only tasting beauty
with my trembling questions,
a seasoned traveller through time
on my breath alone.

KEEPING TIME

Most days I wonder where time goes,
if there will ever be enough of it
to live and to love in all the ways I must.

Sometimes I try to outrun the beat
of my own heart or brace for what's coming,
neither in nor out of it.

Other times I know there is nothing I can do
to stop its unfolding, that this, not death,
is the price of being here.

Now and again, though, I remember to rest,
that in between every beat is a stillness:
miss it and you miss the music.

Guard it with your life so that when you are done
you will know you are in the right place,
in and out of time.

EYEWITNESS

I see you sit down,
run your hand
over your head,
sigh and look up.
Another man walks by,
the river runs in front,
all of us wed now,
as she is our witness.

I wonder if you know
she knows you too,
to speak your heart
before it's too late.
For certain one day
you and I will be dead,
but she will run and run.

I imagine what it's like
at the heart of your world,
the luck, hurts and joys
delivering you here, now,
with those eyes. You,
a man by a river
with his head
in his hands.

SWEET SILENCE

EVERYTHING IS SOFTER AFTER SNOW, sharp urban edges recast in wordless white. The city's heartbeat slows, it's rhythmic breath cold and fresh. Sweet silence blankets, beckons me.

DIVERGENT

a self-portrait

I'm not sure when it happened,
when I stopped being her,
and became me,
all self-doubt and confusion.

Sometimes she held my hands
amongst the trees or in the
trance of the dancefloor.

She spoke to me in tongues
in my dreams, leaving yearning,
a map for buried treasure.

If only I knew then
what I know now,
that what is lost
is always found: me,
underfoot for so long,
chanced upon again
in the smile of the familiar
stranger who beckons me home.

FIRST LIGHT

In that sacred moment
between the healing reprieve of darkness
and coming into being,
time collapses into glorious inevitability.

I am ready, alive to possibility,
a gasp away from revival.

REUNION

The sharp edge of my attention,
blunted by years and waning ambition,
rests in me now.

The horizon a destination no longer,
the sum of my affections,
another cause for delight.

I sit in quiet,
ecstatic awe
of the world.

THE CALL

Ring out now, don't hesitate.
You are born for these times.
The whole world is on fire,
there's no room for self-doubt.

You change worlds unseen
just by risking your heart.
Unlock the cage of another
and leave no heart behind.

Remember,
you are a signal,
a siren, a call to prayer.

Let yourself ring out now,
beautiful and dangerous,
through a desperate despairing world.

ACKNOWLEDGEMENTS

Reunion Songs was written across many lands, predominantly Yuggera Turrbal Country and Gumbaynggirr Country, Australia and The Netherlands. I am deeply grateful to the Traditional Custodians of these ancient lands on which these poems were written, and I pay my respects to their Elders throughout time.

I also give thanks to the other-than-human world that these poems were written for and with. My deepest appreciation for their wisdom, patience, kindness and love. Deepest of bows to the Moreton Bay Figs, the Maiwar (Brisbane River) and my feathered friends that gave me shelter and kept me company and close to myself over these last couple of years. It's a privilege to live and create on and with this beautiful land, for which I am deeply grateful.

I also honour my ancestors, the generations of my people from various regions including Éire (Ireland), the English Midlands, London, Northeastern Scotland, Heiligenhafen and Danzig/Gdańsk who held me through my many migrations and carried me here to the shores of this life.

My deepest appreciation to those who read and responded to these poems online, where they first appeared in draft form. Thank you for your friendship and encouragement and for helping me find the courage to imagine this book was possible. I am particularly grateful for the camaraderie and wisdom of the guides and fellow light writers of Martha Beck's Write into Light and the 24hr Cafe. Shout out to fearless singer and vocal coach Mel Lathouras for helping me embody my voice and discover the musicality in my work.

Thank you to the talented folks who assisted with the book, helping to make it beautiful to hold and behold: Caitilin Punshon, Silke Stein, Sophie White and Shane Drinkwater.

I would like to acknowledge the poem 'It's Not Too Late' by Mary Walker, and her workshop of the same name, as inspirations for my poem 'It's Never Too Late', along with the magical container Shamanic Poetry, created by Emma Campbell Webster and Schuyler Brown, where my poem 'It's Time' first made itself known to me.

First and last, my deep love to my family. To my parents for providing such a rich and solid ground for me and my dreams. To Mum for introducing me to the mystery from the very beginning. To my 'Uncle' Don for giving me the use of his studio when I desperately needed space to write. To my husband Kees for his love and encouragement and for always having my back. To Daphne, our daughter, for her love, wisdom and inspiration for me to be more of myself. Thank you also and always to my animal family, without whom I might never have had the courage to connect with my more-than-human kin.

Amanda is a writer, poet and songwriter. Born and raised in the bush outside the city of Brisbane, Australia, she spent most of her adult life far from home, including six years in the middle of nowhere.

She now lives close to where she started, on unceded Yuggera Turrbal Country, with her husband, daughter and animal family.

Visit Amanda's website to join her free poetry subscription.

www.amandacooke.com

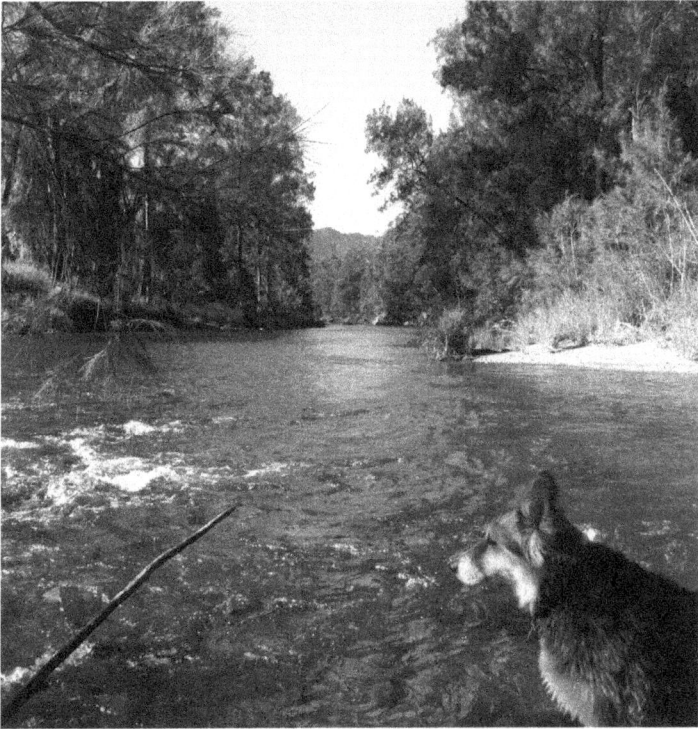

PHOTO CREDITS

[Page 15] *'Sweet Precipitation'*. Darkwood Farm, Gumbaynggirr Country, Thora, Australia. Photo © Amanda Cooke. February 8, 2017.

[Page 25] *'My Morning Meditation'*. Darkwood Farm, Gumbaynggirr Country, Thora, Australia. Photo © Amanda Cooke. March 16, 2017.

[Page 61] *'Sunrise with Toffee'*. Darkwood Farm, Gumbaynggirr Country, Thora, Australia. Photo © Amanda Cooke. February 24, 2016.

[Page 81] *'Sweet Silence'*. Brouwersgracht, Amsterdam, The Netherlands. Photo © Amanda Cooke. December 11, 2017.

[Page 87] *'Dusk Flight'*. Darkwood Farm, Gumbaynggirr Country, Thora, Australia. Photo © Amanda Cooke. August 18, 2017.

[Page 91] *'Under Your Skirt'*. Yuggera Turbal Country, Brisbane, Australia. Photo © Amanda Cooke. February 7, 2023.

[Page 95] *'Sugar'*. Bellinger River, Darkwood Farm, Gumbaynggirr Country, Thora, Australia. Photo © Amanda Cooke. May 6, 2012.